Another Chance

Another Chance

By Annie R Monroe

Copyright

Printed in the United States of America

First Printing, 2015

Second Printing, 2020

ISBN-13: 978-1-942022-21-3

ISBN10: 1942022212

The Butterfly Typeface Publishing
PO BOX 56193
Little Rock Arkansas
72215

Dedication

This book is dedicated to all who have lost loved ones or are coming to terms with tragedy.

All answers are not clearly known on this side of eternity; however, life's meaning can be revealed and lived fully through the knowledge of God.

This book is also dedicated to my college English professor, Dr. Gladys Rosser who encouraged me to express myself through speech.

Dr. Rosser paid very close attention to detail while grading my papers so that she could provide constructive feedback which assisted in bringing me to this place today.

"If you're never scared, or embarrassed, or hurt, it means you never take any chances."

Julia Sorel

Table of Contents

Foreword

This book is life affirming. Never have I felt so pained, yet so liberated. Reading the story of Annie Monroe's life left me feeling a renewed sense of gratification for my own life. I walked away with further confirmation of God's grace and mercy. Another Chance is a story for all people whether you have lost loved ones or if you need to be reminded that life truly is not 'for a lifetime' and that it should not be taken for granted. Kudos Mrs. Monroe for courageously and so poetically sharing your life with the world!

Iris M Williams
Publisher

Acknowledgments

I would like to thank God first,
who has given me this golden
opportunity to share His love and
desire for all people to know Him.

I also pay special tribute to the late
James and Prunell Monroe, my
wonderful parents, for all of the
moral values that they instilled in
me. They labored tirelessly,
mentally and physically, alongside
of me until I was able to see
meaning in my life. After I arrived
at that point, they still carried me
with their presence.

I thank Pastor Pauline Daniels for
the spiritual launching pad she
provided for me long ago.

I want to thank my sons for having
faith in me and believing that their

Mom can make it through anything.

I want to thank all of those who propelled me to this place, knowingly and unknowingly.

Lastly, I thank my lovely publisher, Iris M. Williams, for bringing life to my story and revealing that we, too, share a kindred spirit.

Annie R Monroe

Making Sense of Life

Has a major event ever challenged you to live your life to the fullest?

Many people on this earth have probably not considered the fragility of life. One small mishap, one careless decision, or one seemingly unimportant detail can alter life as we know it now.

There are countless multitudes of individuals that would make the statement, "If I had it to do all over again, I would." Hopefully, that ill-fated statement will encourage you to be mindful of the multitude of blessings you already possess and challenge you to make choices that will improve your life or accept what you cannot change and allow the grace of God to make the best of what remains.

Some lives are lived with ease, some are lived with difficulty, some are lived with challenges, and then there are some that are lived with making the best of shattered pieces. As one that has returned from the brink of death and lived to tell about it, life is best lived as if each day will be the last!

With all of the crooks and turns that life has to offer, who knows what to expect? Who can honestly say without trepidation that life is fair? Why do bad things happen to seemingly undeserving people? These questions will puzzle humanity and go unanswered satisfactorily till the end of the ages.

If anyone should have a beef with life, I personally thought that I qualified many times over. Neither I or nor anyone else can contend with Life; it is so much bigger than you or I and Life has the final say.

Coming to grips with the things I could not change and making the best of the things that remained seemed to be the most viable option. At least it gave me a starting point in trying to make sense of life...

Early Life

I came from a large family that included seven other siblings and was fortunately raised by loving parents. My brothers and sisters and I were taught strict morals and respect which was the norm coming from the South in the 1960's. I grew up with four sisters and three brothers and I never forgot the way that I was raised: to be a hard, honest worker, to be truthful in all of my dealings, to be clean and decent and be a good keeper of the home, to be a good cook, and always respect my elders. I was so afraid to disrespect my elders that anything they said to me, I would never disagree with them.

My mother always taught us that if you honored your elders and those who had authority over us, that we would live a long time. I have always upheld that principle as sacred even as a child and if my longevity depended upon that rule alone, I would probably be the oldest human on earth. My parents also taught my siblings and me to work hard and honestly. In doing so, we would learn to appreciate all that we acquire and learn the value of stewardship and accountability.

I learned later in life that my parents were right and the A-B-C's of honesty and hard work will carry anyone wherever they want to go. But sometimes in our best living, unexpected things in life occur and can take us "through a loop".

As a child, I had a good life, nothing extravagant or over the top, only necessities. Fortunately, my family could afford some luxuries that were mostly non-existent in our neighborhood at that time, like a color television and a telephone. We never allowed these indulgences to get in the way of our family time though. We continued to play kick ball and softball because there were enough of us to make up a team. To me, at that time, I was living in a virtual paradise. No cares… No worries… Just blissfulness. Family, fun, laughter…. the good life was the order of the day.

I had a quick mind and could understand easily once I started school. People said that I got that ability from my Dad, I don't know. I only knew that I loved learning new things and bringing it home and teaching it to my younger siblings. All through grade school, my class assignments came easy to me and I breezed through with great anticipation of what was next for me to learn.

When I got to high school, I still had a firm grasp upon learning except now Math was getting more difficult. When algebra and geometry were introduced, I thought that portion of math was so unimportant and that I would never need to know that, so why did it come along and mess my good record up? I managed to make it through high school however, but my overall average was sadly crippled because of a Pythagorean Theorem. How will I ever use a hypotenuse? I could barely say those terms, let alone understand them.

At that time, I wished I could have met the guy that made the statement that Math was fun. Anyway, my high school graduation could not come quick enough. Although my brain was fried, I was still in one piece and no worse for wear.

I heard about God practically all of my life. My parents were Christians and they took my siblings and me to church every Sunday. But I never knew God personally until I experienced a split second life changing encounter that put a face on the One who had control of my life. After that moment of reckoning, I don't just know about God through all that I heard about Him in church. I now know Him in an intimate way through the powerful manifestation of His Love and Mercy.

Finally an Adult

I never really thought about college which seemed like a luxury back then. Getting your high school diploma was an accomplishment within itself coming from my family and background. There was not a single college graduate that I knew of from my heritage. So having acquired a high school diploma would assure that I could get a job and earn a living, no matter how menial it might be. Finally becoming an adult brought a sense of independence. I can now channel that bit of a rebel that I had bottled within me for so long.

As a child, I never talked back to my parents or authority figures, but now, at least, I can express my approval or disapproval concerning matters. The world is now my oyster where I can explore and make my own way. No restraints, no limitations…. I AM GROWN!!!! Do you hear me world? Open your gates and welcome me because I'm coming!

I lived every moment as someone on a quest to discover every drop of life that was to be gleaned from this planet. I traveled up and down the east coast, exposed myself to a variety of things and people. In all of my explorations, drugs were not of interest to me so I did not experiment with getting my feet wet in that scene. Alcohol and cigarettes were my validation that I was now a grown-up.

Between traveling, working, and partying, I came to the conclusion that this is what life is all about. Deep in the recesses of my soul while I was taking the world by storm, I never did forget the many things my parents taught me while I was a child.

These moral, righteous teachings constantly beckoned to me while I was making my personal mark on the world. Their echoes were ever so gentle and soothing yet their truths reverberated loud and clear piercing my very soul. But not now; I had so much living to do. Maybe later after I'm done checking out what this big world has to offer me with its never-ending smorgasbord of people, places, and pleasures.

Time to Settle Down

Chasing rainbows and fantasies in the world can get old fast. Learning that history repeats itself and there is nothing new under the sun, makes the world a much smaller place.

When I was in my early twenties, I fell in love, married a wonderful man, and had two baby girls. By now I had written algebra and geometry off as ancient history and was enjoying life. I had an older son prior to my marriage and my husband loved him dearly as well.

The ideal future I had in mind for my beautiful family was to enjoy every minute of life and not look back. I was young, intelligent, healthy, and made friends easily. However, before I even started my exciting journey down this unknown path called "happily married" life and live this marvelous vision for my future that I had created, my world would turn upside down.

The portion that wasn't turned upside down was shattered. Totally obliterated and eternally altered! I was immediately transferred to a part of life that is unknown, unbearable, unfamiliar, and unheard of in a matter of hours.

Life would never again be as I had anticipated.

Another Chance | Annie Monroe p. 32

Bump in the Road

My life changed forever on June 22, 1978 after my husband and I had recently celebrated our 2 ½ year wedding anniversary. Also, about two weeks earlier, I had started work at a textile plant where my husband was employed. Having the same shift, we rode to work together after dropping the kids off and then picked them up again after work.

On that fateful day in 1978, we picked the girls up as usual but allowed my son to go fishing with my dad. We spent some time with my relatives, and left about an hour before dark to go home. As we were traveling the nine miles to our home, I fell asleep thinking about how I still had to bathe the babies and getting them ready for bed before I could call it a night. In my half dazed-mind, I pictured the outfits that I would lay out to put on them in the morning to save some time.

 A week or so later, I was told that about one mile from home, my husband ran off the right shoulder of the road on a curve, overcorrected which caused the car to flip then land upside down in a canal ditch. I was also told that my eighteen-month-old daughter was thrown clear of the vehicle, and killed instantly. I was told that when rescue workers arrived at the scene, they removed my husband from the wreckage, rushed him to the hospital and that it took approximately a half hour to free my six-month-old daughter from the wreckage who had also died instantly as a result of a brain contusion.

I was *told* all of this because I was knocked unconscious and have no memory to this day of what happened. I was told that as the workers worked feverishly to free my six-month old baby and my husband from the wreckage, they observed no life in me, and, determining that I was already dead, they took a rest break. Whether I was temporarily deceased or not, I'll never know but I do remember screaming, "help me!" and immediately afterwards, I fell unconscious again.

The next thing I remember was when a doctor was pounding a metal drain tube in my upper chest. I was coming out from under the anesthesia when I felt the excruciating pain but I could not utter a word. Then the same excruciating pain was felt again as another tube was driven in on the other side of my chest. I went unconscious again. Many hours later, I woke up in the intensive care unit with tubes, piping, monitors, and everything possible that I could be hooked up to.

I did not know if I was dead or alive. As a matter of fact, I did not know *who* or *where* I was. I didn't know anything. Later on, I was told that I stared blankly at everyone and moaned constantly due to the severity of my injuries. I was also told about the extent of my injuries which I could not fathom at the time because of temporary amnesia from a head injury. Of course, relatives tried to delay telling me for the longest time the fact that I no longer had a family.

I remember being in an oxygen tent apparatus with oxygen blowing directly into my nostrils to help me breathe while my collapsed lungs had time to heal. I could not talk when I got the devastating news of the death of my family members. I had this large tube in my throat from an emergency tracheotomy from contracting pneumonia.

Another Chance | Annie Monroe p.38

Life-Changing Catastrophe

It would be many weeks
later before I could wrap my mind
around the fact that I no longer had a
wonderful husband and two beautiful
little girls. I was gripped on the inside
with a feeling of an assault on
innocence. What did I do to deserve
this? However, I lay motionless in the
intensive care unit for days, not able to
recognize my own mother.

I was told later that my chances of
survival were slim when I arrived at the
hospital. As six ribs were broken on
my left side, they ripped up my left
kidney. In addition, my liver was split,

my spleen had to be removed, and my nose had to be packed so that it could be sown back together. I sustained an eye injury and a severe head injury with memory loss. I had multiple cuts and gashes on the outside of my body. After surgery to stop the internal bleeding and stabilize my remaining organs, I contracted pneumonia and a tracheotomy had to be performed so that I could breathe. My prognosis did not look good and at the time, my condition was critical.

The request from the doctors was for the family members who visited me in the hospital to not inform me that my husband and baby daughters had perished in the car accident. After about a week, when I was told of their fate, I remember thinking that someone else WAS with me before I ended up in this place, but for the life of me, I couldn't put it all together.

After my condition was updated to critical, but stable, the family broke the news to me about the others and that they had already had the funerals. I remember a stabbing feeling in my chest and it was like all life had drained out of me. I was heart-broken and the tears began to flow hot upon my cheeks. I could not speak because the trachea apparatus was still in my throat allowing me to breathe. I felt as if I would die. My beautiful daughters, I would see no more. My loving husband was not there to comfort me because he was among the casualties.

Beside all that, they were gone and I could not as much as say good-bye for the last time or attend their funerals. I was at the lowest point in my life. I wanted to die myself.

Fortunately, I drifted off a while later from the heavy sedation to the land of forgetfulness. As so I thought. Maybe after I woke up, this terrible dream would be ended and I could get on with my life with my family in tow.

Nightmare in Broad Daylight

I was awakened later that day in excruciating pain. When I opened my eyes, I had visitors waiting for me. They tried to cheer me, but somewhere in a remote chasm of my mind, I relived the conversation informing me that my family was dead.

Sometimes, a million thoughts can cross your mind in a matter of minutes, but this one thought stuck like super glue in the chasm of my mind, "Your family is dead." I tried to search the faces of my visitors for any telltale sign that I was mistaken for thinking such a thing. I read only hurt, sadness, and pity for me as they tried to disguise their true feelings with small talk.

Still unable to speak, one of the visitors seemingly knew what I would have asked if I would have been able to utter a sentence. He pulled out some pictures of my husband and daughters in their coffins. They had just come from the funerals. Gently, they tried to explain the events of the day to me as best and compassionate as they could.

When I saw the coffins with my beautiful angels in them, everything around me paused for a few seconds. I did not know how to feel when I saw the girls with pink, lacy dresses on and pink ribbons in their hair lying motionless in a silk draped coffin.

I stared blankly at the faces that were watching me to see if the whole episode was too overwhelming for me. I could not keep the pictures right now. I could not look at them for the second time. Not right now. This was too much for me to absorb.

Seemingly every cell in my body was aching, if cells can ache from what I had just seen. In a million years, I could not prepare for what has happened and the place I was now occupying. I tried to piece the whole scenario together. My family had just been buried and all I had were some photos of them in the worst form of memory for me. Words could not express the void I experienced as I wept silently. The breathing tube in my throat kept me from wailing out loud as an expression that I was feeling deep down in my very soul.

Somehow my visitors knew by instinct that I now needed to be alone for now. They wanted to stay and comfort me, but there was no comfort. Nothing can be said right now to help me. I love them for being there for me at this critical time of revelation, but it is what it is and it happened to me.

Will I ever be right? Will I ever be able to go on? If I pulled through this, would I want to go on? So many questions and not one answer. If I could just know why, I believe that answer would tide me over for at least one more day. But I had nothing, absolutely nothing but a broken body and a shattered world. How can I live? How can anyone expect me to live? Why should I even want to live? Why was I even born to end up like this?

If I had a say in the matter, my only wish would be to have never existed so that I would not have come to such an unthinkable collision with death and sadness like I now find myself.

WHY? I only wanted to know why? What deep, dark evil did I ever commit to cause such a life changing event? As I searched the annals of my mind, I recanted my whole life in what seemed like an eternity, seeking to uncover that one evil I committed to bring my life to a sudden, dismal halt.

Another Chance | Annie Monroe p. 48

What Now?

Here I am now… a 25-yr. old female with a very young child. A family of five now dwindled to a family of two in a matter of three hours!

What was I supposed to do now?

The memories of my family cannot be erased. What we had could not be forgotten. I am not programmed to delete the past and wipe the memory card clean as if they had never existed.

How could I go on?

It is true that I had a network of loving family, in-laws, and friends who felt pity for me more than anything else. How could they possibly know what I was experiencing?

They offered all kinds of assistance, but nothing could bring my dear family back.

I've heard of dreadful stories far away where multiple family members were lost at one time, but not in my wildest imagination would I have thought that it would happen to me!

Another Chance | Annie Monroe p. 52

Painful Memories

It is impossible to put in words the anguish and torment I endured in the early stages of my calamity. The physical pain was pure torture. My insides crushed, battered, and ripped up from the tragic car crash. My emotions were all over the place. One moment trying to piece this horrible puzzle together, and the next, questioning how everything got so far from normal.

My mental state was as fragile as my riddled body. I felt like I had been hung out to dry. My worse time was at nighttime, when it was seemingly impossible to cope. When the light of day faded and the shadows of darkness began to rule the night, the realities of pain and loss gripped my spirit.

As memories began to return, there were nights I sat nursing my painful, broken and battered, skeletal body, where I was certain I heard the gentle cry of my six-month-old daughter, Chrystal. She was the sweetest baby I believe that was created. In her brief lifetime, the only time that she would cry was when she needed changing or when she was hungry.

She was so self-sufficient. After being fed and clean, you could place her on a mat and she would be content, smiling and cooing softly. How could I live without that element of completion in my life?

At night I could still see my eighteen-month old daughter, LaShanna, going from one person to the next at the dinner table. Her signature trademark was her long, beautiful black hair. What a princess she was…. How can I shut my mind off so I would not be tormented in the wee hours of the night when everything was so deathly quiet and still? Why should I even remain here on earth? Everything was taken from me in a matter of hours.

Thankfully, I still had my son, Anthony, but the memories of the others remained. I felt like I had been dealt the short end of the deal, not taking away from the love I have for my son, but still, why me? What did I ever do so terrible to deserve all this? With despair being the lesser of two evils, I was now staring utter defeat straight in the eye.

Jesus Loves Me Still

Yet in my darkest hours, I could hear Jesus say, "I came just for you. To hurt like you hurt, to suffer like you suffer, to endure sadness and loneliness like you are experiencing. I came just to carry you through these times."

I do not remember who witnessed to me about salvation; so many godly people were allowed to visit me. Maybe the doctors thought that Pastors and Christians would be good for me at a crucial time as this.

My survival was not etched in stone. I could maintain consciousness for only brief periods of time. I could not recall exactly when it happened, but during one of my periods of consciousness, I repented of my sins and asked Christ to come into my life. There was no grand fanfare or loud shouts in a congregational setting. No words uttered because I could not talk at the time. There were no tears streaming down my face. As a matter of fact, I probable drifted off as soon as I made my declaration of faith as a born-again child of God.

From that moment on, I experienced something that I had never encountered before. In the deepest recesses of my soul, I now know that I had been forgiven and changed from the inside out.

My physical body was still broken and suffering untold pain, but my spirit was free. It was still a fact that my family was gone and I had to make major adjustments if I survived. I learned that a crisis will either bring out the best, or the worst in a person.

Yes, it took me a while to understand that life is uncertain, but I have the choice as to how I live it according to what is dealt to me. I learned that coming to terms with life events (good or bad) and accepting that *it is what it is*, was how a surefire way to developing and living the best life possible with what remained.

Picking Up The Pieces

In the midst of the tragedy that had recently occurred, I could have chosen to be bitter or better. To consider ending it all would be in essence giving in to defeat. I considered all the loved ones I would leave behind to suffer added grief along with the already insurmountable grief they were already facing with the recent tragedy.

That would be selfish and definitely not the answer. Even through insufferable crisis, I learned that no one is immune to trouble. In the package deal of just being born in this world, trouble is one of the inevitable occurrences we all face.

There is a bigger picture of destiny that we all have here on earth but often we miss it because we focus on the here and now. Truthfully, we exploited a lot of opportunities that we have to make the needful adjustments to put ourselves on the right track.

Our destiny is not right before our face; we have to launch out and progress toward that place in the future designed just for us. As I look back over the past events of my life, I can clearly see that I was destined to come to this place so that God could be glorified.

Days passed and my condition began to improve after surgery. I even began to smile and be thankful whereas beforehand, I felt hopeless. My nurses and doctors made it a point to encourage me that my condition was being upgraded once I released the hope and joy I received through salvation.

The trachea tube was removed after about seven days and I began to find my voice once more. The external circumstances had not changed at all, but now I possessed something far more enduring that assisted me in coping with my recent losses. This new-found experience was exciting to me.

Slowly, I began to remember faces and greeted people optimistically. A lot of events I still don't remember, but I joyfully told everyone that I had been born again! Thank God I remembered that! Something alive on the inside of me kept reminding me that I now have a powerful future and eternal life as well.

I would find myself laughing out loud when no one was around because this spiritual transformation gave me hope and it literally changed my death and

doom thoughts to thoughts of life. I
began to realize that I was now going
to live and live a life of joy despite what
has happened.

God gave me a second chance at life
and I was not going to waste it in sin
any longer. When I think about how
close I came to death and the possible
eternal fate that could be awaiting for
me had I died, it really open up my
understanding concerning the love that
God has for all creation. That very
realization prompted me to tell
everyone about the love of God.

I remembered when some people
would come to visit me in the hospital,
they felt sorry for me and did not know
what to say. Thank God, I knew what
to say! I would tell them that
everything was going to be all right
now because I had received Jesus
Christ as my Savior and I invited them
to do the same.

Another Chance | Annie Monroe p.66

Facing Facts

I spent thirty days in the hospital and I grew in my faith every day. My body was weak, broken, tattered, and scarred, but my spirit was free. God allowed me to live when I could have easily perished along with the rest of my family. God gave me another chance at life to proclaim His love toward mankind and to tell people to not wait until tragedy strikes before making life-changing decisions.

I believe within myself that if I had not repented when the Holy Spirit prompted me to while still in the hospital, either one of three things could have possibly happened:

(1) I would have later died because my injuries were conducive to death,

(2) I would have survived with health problems so unfathomable in their severity that I would not have been able to cope and quite possibly sought solace in drugs, alcohol, etc., or quite frankly, committed suicide, or

(3) I could have possibly never come to terms with what has happened and experience a nervous breakdown and become institutionalized with mental problems indefinitely.

But the grace of God prevailed and I am a living witness to the delivering power of God.

At the time, I could not think of anything much more traumatic than losing my two beautiful baby girls and my husband at the same time, except the account of Job in the Old Testament. After Job lost all that he had including his family, Job was smitten with sore boils.

After losing my family and my health at a young age, my very existence had now become uncertain.

Go On From Here

Again, it would be impossible to put in words all that I endured. Through this experience I learned one thing and that fact influences everything here on earth. God is ALL GOOD and Satan is ALL EVIL.

Since the fall of mankind through disobedience in the Garden of Eden, sin has entered this world that we live in. Since Adam, (the first man) sinned, sin is passed on to every person that is born into this world. I have come to realize that we live in a world of sin. Because of my recent tragedy, it was easy for me to blame God for allowing such an event to upset my life. My plans were to have a beautiful family and live happily ever after. But I realized that there is no happily ever after without Christ. Since Satan is the god of this world, as the result of the first sin committed by the first man, Adam, Satan's agenda is to steal, kill, and destroy. My family was taken as a result of Satan, not God. "God is ALL THAT IS GOOD."

God sent His only begotten Son, Jesus, that we might have life and have it more abundantly, to the full, and until it overflows. When I was able to distinguish the difference between good and evil, God and Satan, life and death, it was plain to see who was behind the deaths of my family members.

Satan does not care if it is an innocent baby, his mission is to destroy and cause as much misery, hurt, and pain without any thought of having mercy. But God, on the other hand, had mercy on me even in the midst of this unthinkable tragedy. He cared for me during the time I blamed Him until I came to grips with reality. He cared for me when I felt like giving up and He encouraged me to continue on because life is worth living even with the difficult adjustments I had to make.

When I was deep in despair and blaming God for my misfortune, He continued to have mercy and patience with me until I was convinced through His Word that He has a marvelous plan for my life and that it was not His will that any of my family members perish; it was the design of Satan as the result of sin that they did not survive.

God has a plan to prosper and bless me all the days of my life. God is the One who encouraged me through His Word that all is not lost and that I can make it. When I did a side-by-side comparison, I realized that Satan brought only defeating words to me saying I had nothing to live for. God encouraged me to live by telling me to trust Him to give me a life of peace and victory even in the midst of tragedy. When I understood that Jesus loves me and that He wants what's best for me, it was not hard to believe His Word. Nobody likes a liar. Satan is a liar and he lied to me when he said that I had nothing to live for.

God has healed my body from its physical brokenness. I have not had one treatment for dialysis from the loss of my kidney. My liver is functioning properly. I've had the flu only once from a weakened immune system due to the removal of my spleen.

There are still some things in my past life that I still do not recall, but I am not focused on that. I press forward toward the mark of the high calling of God in Christ Jesus. The past is the past. I cannot change history, but I can make a positive and powerful statement about the future. Not only has God healed me physically, but He has healed my spiritual brokenness.

I do not constantly entertain the fact that my husband and babies are not here and the tragic way in which they left here. I cannot change that. But what I can change is how I think and what I think on. I choose to think on things that are lovely, honest, just, pure, and things of good report. Death is not a good report, but life is. I have a choice to meditate on things that make for peace, righteousness, and life.

All of these mind developing thoughts are contained in the Word of God, the Holy Bible. Although it has been many years since the loss of my family, I am challenged each day to renew my mind by meditating on the Word of God. This renewal changes one's outlook on life and gives hope and stability as well.

Forever Changed

Every time I look at the scars on my body that I will always bear, it is just a constant reminder of the goodness of God. These scars could have been confined forever in the tomb of my demise, but I thank God for giving me the chance to shout from the mountaintops that Jesus is merciful and His mercy endures forever.

Jesus is the Savior of the world! He is the only way to God the Father. Through faith in the name of Jesus, we all can live eternally with God in Heaven! I also realize that these scars, mentally and physically, could have been the means for my earthly passing; however, they are the marks of my new beginning on the road to my spiritual destiny in Christ. Such a small price to pay to awaken me to the reality that Jesus gave His life for you and me. Why think of failure when there is victory in Christ Jesus? Many times I thought, "I can't go on," but I can move forward in Christ Jesus.

I experienced pain, sadness, abandonment, fear, uncertainty, loneliness and I felt defeated, but when I heard about Jesus, then the most dominant belief in my life (my faith) overcame any defeating thought. Even when these pessimistic thoughts come to mind, (and they come to all of us), faith and confession in what the Word of God says about the situation, is assurance of overcoming victory in all things.

Faith comes by hearing, and hearing by the Word of God. With what has happened to me, how can I not revisit the biblical account of Job? My situation was nothing in comparison to all that Job had to endure, but it was my personal account nonetheless.

No one's place of severe testing should ever be minimized or compared to another person's trials and used to make a measuring rod to account for which one is greater. Suffering is real to the one who is enduring the plight and has its own effect on the individual.

Never Alone

Of course I think of my husband and babies from time to time, and my understanding of their brief lives on earth has not been revealed. THINGS DON'T JUST HAPPEN! There is a purpose for all things that happen in your life and mine.

The end of it all is that God loves you and me and His number one purpose for our existence is for us to accept Christ as Lord and Savior, and share our faith so that when this life is over, we all will live eternally with Him in heaven. Life is good after all!

Life is so precious and very, very fragile. Each day with the Lord for me now is a new adventure and it should be that way. Each day should be a day of great expectations and faithful anticipation of what God is revealing to me to hasten me onward toward the earthly destiny that He left me here to fulfill.

Through the years, I have faced many difficult challenges concerning my own mortality and memories of my past family.

Thankfully, while raising my young son, I had a community of supporters that helped and encouraged me as a young believer. But just like the death of a loved one, when the funeral is over, everyone has to go home.

Then it is business as usual but the fact remains that loneliness is still an unwelcome guest that hangs around long past any other guest and literally wears his welcome out. Yet he has packed his bags and is determined to move in permanently.

Loneliness stays for a very short while before his family starts moving in uninvited. You know his brother oppression, his sister hopelessness and there are other family members like doubt and bitterness. I experienced all of these emotions when I was at my most vulnerable point. There are some bridges in life that I had to cross "alone", but God was with me, and in essence, I was never alone.

Emotions are real but they can sometimes hold us captive to defeat if the knowledge of the presence of God is not realized. The absence of my husband and daughters made everyday living seemingly unbearable at times, but there is great comfort in knowing that God will always be there.

That fact of God's presence alone is the motivation that kept me in hope every time I put my son to bed and kissed him goodnight.

Even though I was giving out only one kiss now when a short while ago I was giving out three more became all so surreal to me, but it was not a dream. I was living in real time with a lot of adjustments to make.

Still I count it a blessing that I am able to embrace a child and tell him how much I love him.

Another Chance | Annie Monroe p. 86

Acceptance Through Grace

I am reminded in scripture to press forward toward the "higher call" of God, but admittedly, sometimes I find myself stuck. Stuck with unanswered questions and occasionally emptiness in the pit of my stomach.

After all, I did embrace two daughters that are no more, with the detachment of the whole mother-daughter scenario. But, here again, I have to consciously and purposely bring my focus back to the here and now.

I console myself in relishing the memories of my daughters and the fleeting moments that we shared and look forward to the day that I will see them again.

God did not pick flowers for His garden when the appointed time for my daughters had come. In His sovereign wisdom, it was already predestined the determined days for me to spend with my daughters.

This thought alone has prompted me to never take loved ones and life itself for granted. This precious sojourn each of us have on this side of eternity is to be treasured and shared each day. In all honesty to myself, I cannot truthfully say that I have closure no matter how long it has been. I call it acceptance.

I could never close a portion of my life that had been so much a part of me but I have learned to accept that which I cannot change and move forward.

The poignant memories still carry a stinging sensation from time to time as they awaken what once was a vibrant part of my family circle.

But the good thing about wounds is that they eventually heal although some leave everlasting scars. I have used my physical scars as a reminder of the mercy of God.

His Love is from everlasting to everlasting.

God, Family,
Friends, Life

While you have everything that is dear to you by your side, seek the Lord. You may have a beautiful family, a great job, good friends, and a healthy body, all that you could ask for.

When we possess all that we love, that is the prime time to receive Christ as Savior.

We don't know what tomorrow will bring. It could bring sunshine or rain. No one can accurately predict what will happen each day because things can change in an instant.

I am a prime candidate to testify that you can be on cloud nine today and instantly sink to the pits of hopelessness before the sun goes down.

If we live for any length of time on this earth, sadness is coming to us all. That's the nature of this world we live in.

But we have hope in Christ Jesus that when that time comes, we can rely on Christ to guide us to His marvelous purpose despite the circumstances.

While the blood is still coursing warm in your veins, accept Christ Jesus as your personal Savior. He will exchange your ashes for beauty and cause you to be that person that someone is desperately waiting to hear from.

You have been assigned to help someone in this life.

I beseech you to start your journey to your powerful destiny by saying yes to Christ and see Him cause you to rise to heights that you never thought possible.

Life is good after all!

Another Chance

As I continue to make my trek through this journey called life, I constantly make new and amazing discoveries about the Grace of God. I don't deserve life; no one does. But the very essence of the love of God compels me to seek Him out and tell of His goodness.

His mercies are fresh and abundant every day. My thought life is still intact and over the years, I have constant reminders of my loss through the loss of others, but now I am able to assist in the grief process and offer hope in Christ.

The underlying fact is that there is hope beyond despair; there is hope beyond sadness and loss. That hope can only be found in Jesus, the Christ.

I have been granted *another chance* to enjoy the life that God has purposed for me and to fulfill my destiny.

The realization came at an unspeakable cost; but, nevertheless, the message is loud and clear.

Seek the Lord while He may be found. Love God with all of your heart, mind, soul, body, and strength and your neighbor as yourself. Love your family and make it a point to tell them verbally that you love them.

A lot of socio-backgrounds do not have a rich heritage of expressing love to family members verbally because it was not shown or taught in the homes.

Some individuals have never heard their parents tell each other "I love you." But a conscious effort has to be made to say those life-changing words, ("I love you"), to add the substance that keep families together.

A Gratitude Journal

Learn to appreciate life, family, friends, and all the good things that have been provided to make existence here on earth enjoyable. Make it a priority to tell your family and friends how much you love and appreciate them. For certain, the day is coming when our circle of family and friends will be broken and it will be impossible to express our love to one who cannot return our heartfelt adoration with a smile, a hug, or a nod of acceptance.

Lavish love on one another every day because when our loved one's voices are silenced, our hearts can find peace in knowing that while they were here, love was the principle thing.

Live life to the fullest because Jesus came that we may have and enjoy our lives in abundance, to the fullest, until it overflows.

On these next few pages, take some time to reflect on all of the wonderful things God has done in your life.

When we can think positively, we can begin to live in that manner as well.

Gratitude Journal

Gratitude Journal

Gratitude Journal

_____

_____

_____

_____

_____

Gratitude Journal

_____

_____

_____

_____

_____

_____

Gratitude Journal

Gratitude Journal

_____

_____

_____

_____

_____

_____

Gratitude Journal

_____

_____

_____

_____

_____

Gratitude Journal

_____

_____

_____

_____

_____

_____

Gratitude Journal

Gratitude Journal

_____

_____

_____

_____

_____

_____

Gratitude Journal

Gratitude Journal

_____

_____

_____

_____

_____

_____

Gratitude Journal

_____

_____

_____

_____

_____

Gratitude Journal

Gratitude Journal

_____

_____

_____

_____

_____

Gratitude Journal

_____

_____

_____

_____

_____

_____

Gratitude Journal

_____

_____

_____

_____

_____

_____

Gratitude Journal

_____

_____

_____

_____

_____

_____

Gratitude Journal

Gratitude Journal

_____

_____

_____

_____

_____

_____

Gratitude Journal

Gratitude Journal

_____

_____

_____

_____

_____

Gratitude Journal

Suggestions for Overcoming Grief

Remember to **PACE** *yourself:*

Pray (talk to God and ask for His help and guidance)

Allow (don't ignore your feelings, allow yourself time to feel them)

Cry (it is ok to cry, crying helps release pain)

Express (talk to others and write down your feelings in a letter or journal)

Scriptures to help you cope with grief

"To all who mourn…he will give: beauty for ashes; joy instead of mourning; praise instead of heaviness. For God has planted them like strong and graceful oaks for his own glory."

Isaiah 61:3TLB

"Blessed be the God…of all comfort, who comforts us in all our tribulation, that we may be able to comfort those who are in any trouble, with the comfort with which we ourselves are comforted by God."

2 Corinthians 1:3-4 NKJV

"He will once again fill your mouth with laughter and your lips with shouts of joy."

Job 8:21 NLT

Scriptures to help you cope with grief

"The ransomed of the Lord will return. They will enter Zion with singing; everlasting joy will crown their heads. Gladness and joy will overtake them, and sorrow and sighing will flee away."

Isaiah 35:10 NIV

"He turned my sorrow into joy! He took away my clothes of mourning and clothed me with joy."

Psalm 30:11 TLB

"May our Lord Jesus Christ himself and God our Father, who loved us and by his grace gave us eternal comfort and a wonderful hope, comfort you and strengthen you.

2 Thessalonians 2:16-17 NLT

About the Author

Annie R. Monroe was born in Raeford, North Carolina to James and Prunell Monroe. She was born in a family of seven other siblings and grew up in a humble and loving home. She is a graduate of Hoke County High School in Raeford, North Carolina.

She received an Associates in Cosmetology from Sandhills Community College and worked as a Cosmetologist for twelve years. She later went back to school and graduated Magna Cum Laude from Shaw University, Raleigh, North Carolina, with a Bachelors of Arts degree in Sociology.

She worked five years as a Mental Health Qualified Professional for persons with mental health and substance abuse diagnoses. She also worked in the field of education for thirteen years as a teacher's assistant in positions ranging from Pre-K-Exceptional Children's Programs.

Ms. Monroe is a church elder and adult Sunday School teacher. She is very active in her church in other offices as well.

One of Ms. Monroe's greatest joys is visiting rest homes and sharing the joy of the Lord with the residents.

Affirming that she got her "green thumb" from her mother; Ms. Monroe also enjoys making living floral baskets and delivering them to the elderly, the sick, and the home-bound.

Ms. Monroe thrives on bringing happiness to the downcast, the forgotten, the underdog, the downtrodden, and the hopeless.

The mother of four sons, Ms. Monroe is therefore an avid sports fan and cook. One specialty bakery item that everyone loves is her Amish bread which she bakes regularly and distributes mainly at Christmastime each year to family, friends, and the sick and shut-in.

Ms. Monroe is also the proud grandmother of three "grandsugars," AJ, Taliyah, and Robert III.

Committed to teach the gospel, Ms. Monroe is inspired to lift and encourage people in a time such as this.

Author Contact

Ms. Monroe would love to hear from you!

You may email the author at:

anotherchancebook@gmail.com

Contact The

Butterfly Typeface Publishing

for all your

publishing & writing needs!

Iris M Williams
PO Box 56193
Little Rock AR 72215
501-681-0080

the Butterfly Typeface